FAR *from* SHORE

Chronicles of an Open Ocean Voyage

For my parents, Nancy and Bill Webb

Houghton Mifflin Books for Children is an imprint of
Houghton Mifflin Harcourt Publishing Company.

www.hmhbooks.com

Book design by YAY! Design
The text of this book is set in Perpetua.
The illustrations are watercolor, gouache, and graphite.

Library of Congress Cataloging-in-Publication Data

Webb, Sophie.
  Far from shore : chronicles of an open ocean voyage /
written and illustrated by Sophie Webb.
    p. cm.
  ISBN 978-0-618-59729-1
  1. Dolphins—Counting—Pacific Ocean—Juvenile
literature. 2. Sea birds—Counting—Pacific Ocean—
Juvenile literature. 3. Marine animals—Research—
Pacific Ocean—Juvenile literature. 4. Webb, Sophie—
Travel—Pacific Ocean—Juvenile literature. I. Title.
  QL737.C432W427 2011
  591.77'4—dc22
                            2010025121

Printed in China
LEO 10 9 8 7 6 5 4 3 2 1

4500275256

FAR *from* SHORE

Chronicles of an Open Ocean Voyage

Sophie Webb

Houghton Mifflin Books for Children
Houghton Mifflin Harcourt
Boston New York 2011

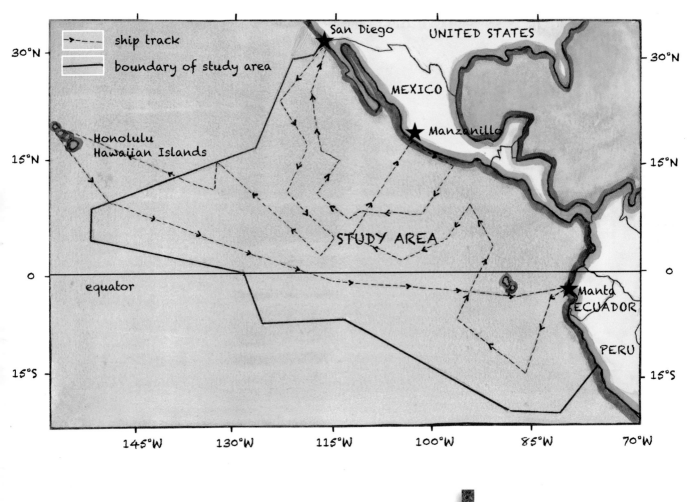

The part of the Eastern Tropical Pacific (ETP) where I will travel on this cruise to study marine mammals and seabirds.

My name is Sophie. I work as a field biologist and naturalist specializing in birds. Tomorrow I am going on a four-month journey to the Eastern Tropical Pacific Ocean (ETP) to study seabirds and marine mammals. I work for the Southwest Fisheries Science Center, a research laboratory run by the National Oceanic and Atmospheric Administration (NOAA) in California. The cruise's main goal is to discover what has happened to dolphin populations that have been affected by the tuna purse-seine fishery. However, we will also observe and count all other marine mammals that we encounter, count the seabirds (my main job), make oceanographic measurements, and study flying fish and squid. As scientists we want to understand the ecosystem as a whole, not only one part. The ETP, where we will work, is a huge portion of the Pacific, the world's largest ocean. It extends south from California to Peru and west to Hawaii, an area of 7.7 million square miles, larger than the continent of Africa.

The open ocean, far from land, can seem lonely and empty, yet there are areas in the ETP that are full of amazing wildlife. Because it is so difficult to study these deep-sea animals far from shore, little is known about their natural history and ecology. My shipmates and I are about to embark on an incredible opportunity to explore this complex and exciting ecosystem.

beaked whales

JULY—SAN DIEGO, CALIFORNIA

32°73′ North latitude, 117°17′ West longitude

I drive south from my home in central California to San Diego. There I spend several days helping load scientific equipment aboard the NOAA ship *McArthur II* and setting up our work areas. Over the flying bridge, the highest deck on the ship, the ship's crew has strung a canvas canopy to provide shade. We will be grateful for the shade as we head south into the sunny tropics.

We've installed four sets of "big eyes," which will be key to our observations. We use these enormous mounted binoculars with a twenty-five-power magnification to scan to the horizon for marine mammals or count distant bird flocks. Three computer stations with chairs are also set up. Two stations, one per side, are where we birders sit to collect our bird data. The third one in the middle is where the marine mammal data recorder sits.

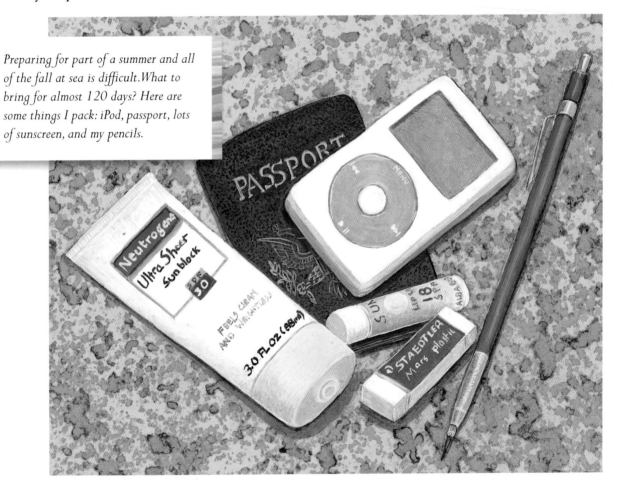

Preparing for part of a summer and all of the fall at sea is difficult. What to bring for almost 120 days? Here are some things I pack: iPod, passport, lots of sunscreen, and my pencils.

There are thirty-seven people on the ship. Fifteen are scientists: one chief scientist, six marine mammal observers, two birders (one of them is me), two oceanographers, and four visiting scientists. The remaining twenty-two aboard include the captain, cooks, engineers, a variety of NOAA officers, who navigate and drive the ship, and the deck department folks, who clean and paint the ship and help us collect our data by driving the small boats and running the cranes and winches for casting nets and other equipment.

I have worked with many of the scientists before and know most of the ship's crew well. I've spent almost two of the past four years living and working on the *McArthur II,* so the first few days are always fun, catching up with others and learning what they have been doing over the months since the last trip.

Although over the next months we will collect data on many aspects of the marine ecosystem, the primary

A bird's-eye view of the flying bridge shows the location of our stations and the big eyes.

bow

marine mammal scientist chair and desk with computer box

big eyes

big eyes

bird scientist chair and desk with computer box

I scan for birds from my chair on the flying bridge.

The dry lab where the computers are located. There is a wet lab as well, with two large sinks, one with fresh water, the other with salt water, where the samples from net tows and other scientific activities are processed.

My stateroom, or cabin, has a bunk bed, a sink, and a desk. The "head," or bathroom, is located between two staterooms, so my cabin-mate, Shannon, and I share it with the stateroom next door. There are twenty-six staterooms on the ship. Some rooms are doubles and are mostly occupied by the scientists. The singles are generally for the officers and crew, who may spend up to twelve months per year living on the ship.

mast for internet connection to satellite

rescue boat

boat used for science

"A" frame to deploy equipment

"J" frame to deploy equipment

labs

staterooms

McARTHUR II

stern

The mess where we have our meals and where we often socialize in the evenings.

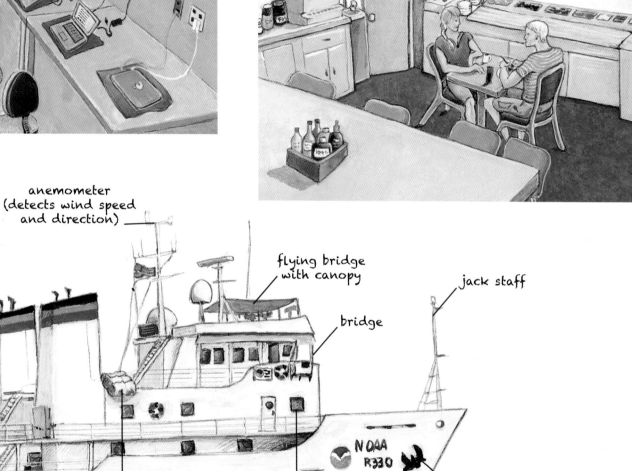

anemometer
(detects wind speed
and direction)

flying bridge
with canopy

jack staff

bridge

NOAA
R330

anchor

mess

captain's cabin

bow

life rafts

focus of the trip is to find out what is happening to the populations of spotted and spinner dolphins.

Why do we want to know about spotted and spinner dolphin numbers? There are several threats to these animals. The primary one used to be the yellowfin tuna fishery. In the ETP, tuna and dolphins are often found in large schools together. Tuna frequently are caught by a method called purse seining. A net is dragged to surround a tuna school, then drawn closed. If there are dolphins with the tuna, they are caught as well. In the past, tens of thousands of dolphins drowned each year in purse seines. This needless loss of life caused a great outcry by the general public and scientists in the 1970s. The result was the formation of the United States Marine Mammal Protection Act, which protects dolphins and other marine mammals in U.S. waters. Now most marine mammals are also protected by international law.

Currently, scientists closely monitor the tuna fishery. Now most tuna fishermen allow the dolphins to escape before they drown, sometimes with a swimmer in the net to help the dolphins escape. But dolphin populations are not recovering as quickly as predicted, and scientists don't know why. Does capture cause stress that lowers their survival? Or perhaps overfishing and pollution combined with shifts in climate may be affecting the balance of the ocean ecosystem. With long-term monitoring, combined with ecosystem studies, we hope to understand why these populations aren't recovering at a faster rate.

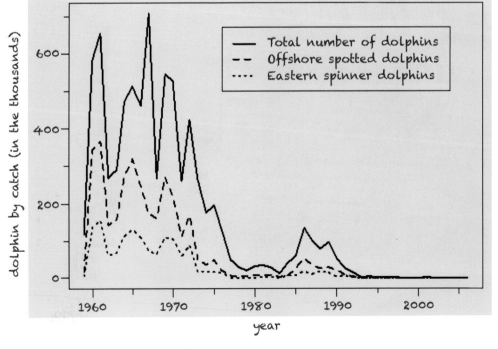

A graph showing how the numbers of dolphins killed in the yellowfin tuna purse-seine fishery has declined.

Courtesy NOAA SWFSC

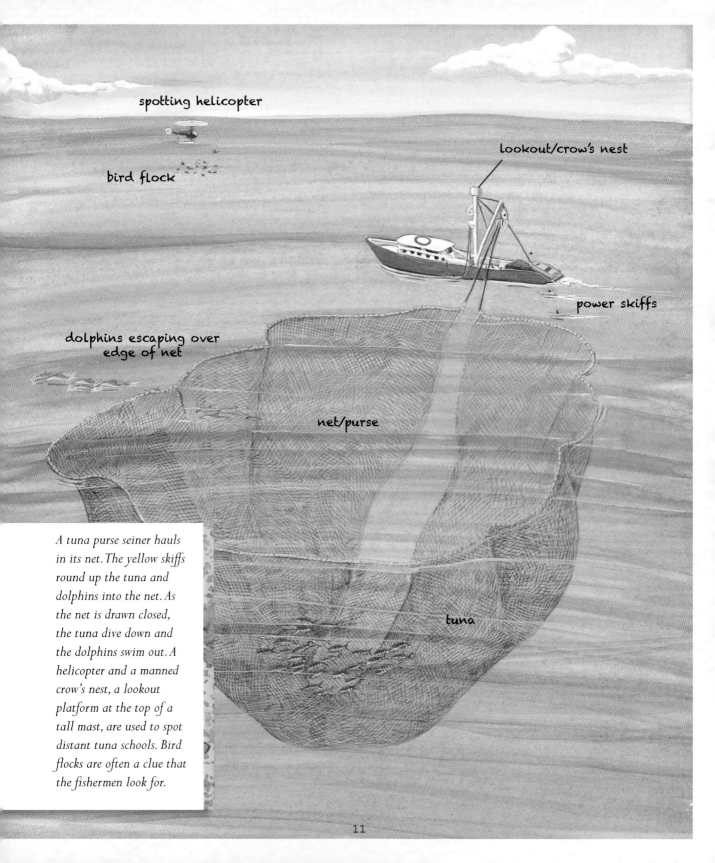

spotting helicopter

bird flock

lookout/crow's nest

power skiffs

dolphins escaping over edge of net

net/purse

tuna

A tuna purse seiner hauls in its net. The yellow skiffs round up the tuna and dolphins into the net. As the net is drawn closed, the tuna dive down and the dolphins swim out. A helicopter and a manned crow's nest, a lookout platform at the top of a tall mast, are used to spot distant tuna schools. Bird flocks are often a clue that the fishermen look for.

Finally we are ready to leave San Diego. Before each long journey there is always a sense of anticipation. What will we see this time? There is, however, a downside to every long trip. I know I will miss my home, family, and friends.

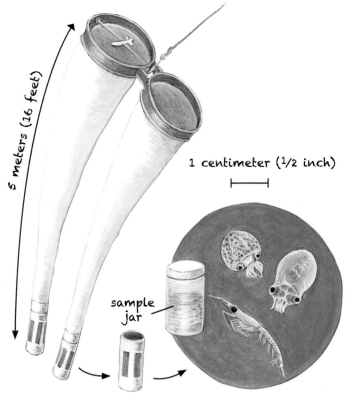

5 meters (16 feet)

1 centimeter (½ inch)

sample jar

cod end collects sample

This net, called a bongo because it looks like the drum, is used for catching small fish and plankton. Some creatures frequently caught in a bongo tow are pictured here clockwise: a spotted larval squid, a semi-clear larval octopus, and a krill. Krill are small relatives of shrimp and are an important food for whales and birds.

HEADING SOUTH
15°47′ N, 120°52′ W

Over the next days we move off shore and head south to warm tropical water. Our route takes us south of the Hawaiian Islands. In a few weeks, after a month at sea, we will turn and head north to Hawaii to resupply and fuel the ship. The ocean color has changed since we left San Diego; it is a beautiful clear blue. I look down through the water and it seems as though I can see for miles. Here the water can be much more than a mile deep. It looks nothing like the ocean near shore off California, which often has a murky green or brownish cast to it caused by lots of plankton and algae. The tropical ocean is clear because it has much less of these.

Where there is food, there are animals. In the tropical ocean animals tend to be found in patches where there is more plankton and algae. Small fish and krill eat the plankton and algae, larger fish and squid eat them, and so on up the food chain to tuna and dolphins. One of the things we want to understand is what causes this patchiness. We combine our marine mammal and seabird observations with measurements of water, plankton, and algae. Every morning an hour before sunrise and every evening an hour after sunset we collect water samples from the surface down to 1,000 meters to look at the water's nutrients and chlorophyll. These nutrients are the building blocks of the ocean food chain. In the evening we also deploy nets to determine the amount and types of plankton at different depths. We use dip nets to catch flying fish and squid. All this information helps us have a more complete picture of the ecosystem of the tropical ocean.

A graph of a water sample showing measurements of oxygen, temperature, and salinity (salt) in the water from the surface to 1,000 meters (3,000 feet). As one follows the graph from 1000 meters to the surface, note the drastic changes at a depth of about 100 meters: oxygen and temperature increase sharply as the salinity decreases. This is where two different water masses meet and is called the thermocline. *A thermocline that is strong and close to the surface (50 to 100 meters) can indicate a highly productive area where we might find not only a large amount of algae and plankton but also animals much higher in the food chain such as tuna and dolphins.* Courtesy NOAA SWFSC

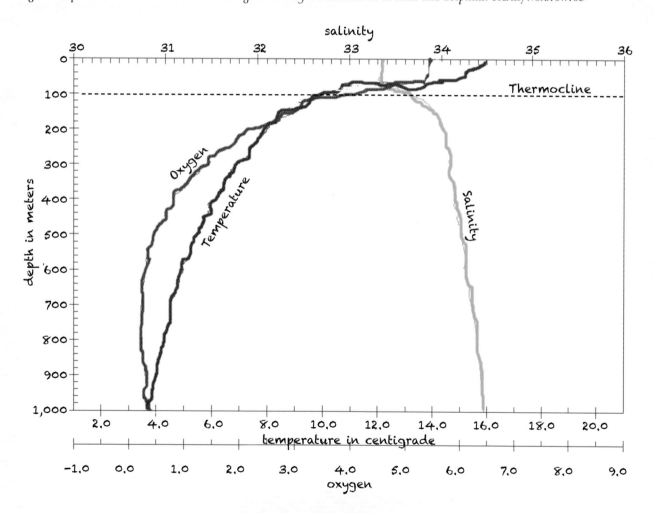

At Beaufort 0, the ocean is glassy calm. One can see for miles. The pink and violet sunrise reflects on the still water.

A DAY OFFSHORE
13°13′ N, 122°47′ W

The day dawns clear and calm, absolutely beautiful. The seas are glassy: Beaufort 0 (a nautical scale that assigns numbers based on wind speed and waves). Observations start just after dawn, when there is enough light to see out to the horizon. Everyone is ready on the flying bridge. Cornelia, a German marine mammal biologist, and Ernesto, a Mexican marine mammal biologist, stand on each side of the flying bridge to scan with the big eyes for marine mammals. Jim, an American marine mammal biologist, sits in the middle at the data computer. I sit with hand-held binoculars on either the port (left) or the starboard (right) side, depending on where I can avoid the sun's glare to scan for birds.

It's time to start looking for critters. It is ten minutes past sunrise and the light is good. We start to travel along a set course, what scientists call a transect. Soon after we start, Cornelia yells, "Dolphins!" All scanning stops and everyone focuses on Cornelia's sighting.

She swings the big eyes in the direction of the dolphins.

Using her hand-held radio, Cornelia calls the captain on the bridge deck below us, where the ship's steering controls are located. "Bridge, flying bridge—we have dolphins," she says. "Please turn twenty degrees to the left. Over." The ship turns.

Cornelia scans out to the horizon, looking through the big eyes.

What Cornelia sees through the big eyes.

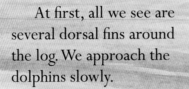

At first, all we see are several dorsal fins around the log. We approach the dolphins slowly.

One brown booby and four Nazca boobies rest on a log surrounded by dolphins. Boobies are often seen far out at sea, resting on any available floating object, including ships and sea turtles.

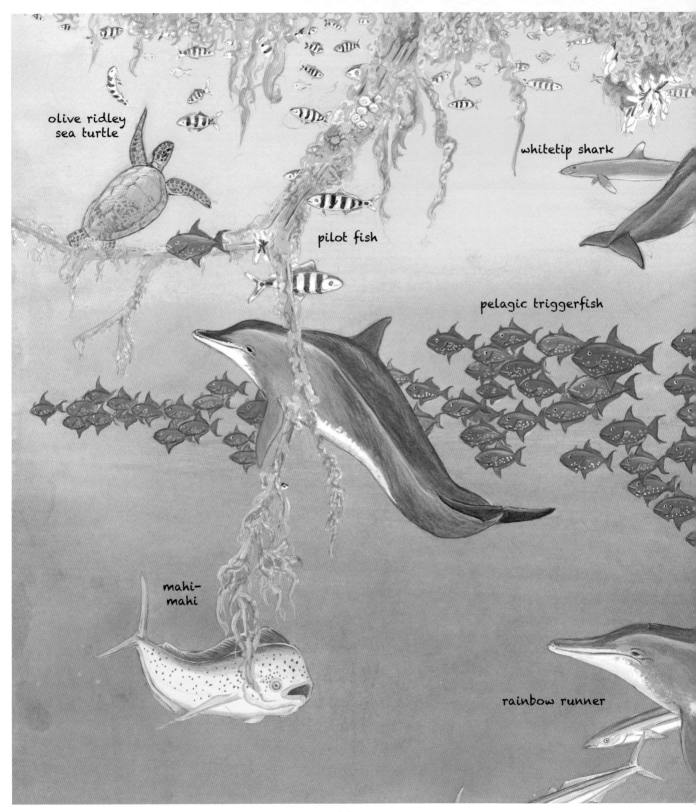

olive ridley
sea turtle

whitetip shark

pilot fish

pelagic triggerfish

mahi-
mahi

rainbow runner

puffer fish

tripletail

rough-toothed
dolphin

Finally we see odd sloped foreheads and long beaks: they are rough-toothed dolphins. This species is found in many oceans. Although relatively common, little is known of their natural history due to their deep ocean habitat. All creatures that inhabit the deep ocean are difficult to study.

The water is so clear, I see subtle markings on the dolphins as they swim by.

What I imagine it looks like below the log. Frequently, rough-toothed dolphins investigate logs, feeding on the fish that hide in the seaweed growing on the log. Many different animals are attracted to the habitat the log creates. Rough-toothed dolphins specialize in eating large fish such as the mahi-mahi.

All dolphins are odontocetes *(toothed whales). Odontocetes also include porpoises, the little-known beaked whales, killer whales, and sperm whales. There is a great variation in size from the tiny harbor porpoise that measures 1.2 meters (4 feet) to the 18.5-meter (60-foot) male sperm whale.*

sperm whale

killer whale (male)

striped dolphin

harbor porpoise

We complete the rough-toothed dolphin count. There are twelve in the group and no calves (babies). Marine mammal biologists always note the presence or absence of calves and immature animals to gain clues about when and where the dolphins reproduce. We leave the dolphins by their log and continue on our course.

The day becomes progressively warmer. The air is still. Everyone is sleepy. The ship drones on along the transect line. We see no more marine mammals now, but birds occasionally fly by, such as the sparrow-size Galápagos storm-petrel. I record birds out to 300 meters (630 feet) on one side of the ship. Even when there are few birds, I have to stay focused and alert. I don't want to miss any of them in my count.

I worry about how climate change, pollution, and overfishing may affect all wildlife in our oceans. Over the years I have spent at sea I have seen more and more plastic and oil pollution, and more entangled animals. I have noted the numbers of some species of seabirds decline. Birds are highly visible both at their breeding colonies on islands and at sea. They are like canaries in a coal mine. When they die in large numbers or are absent from an area where they were normally abundant, they tell us that something has happened in the ocean. The cause could be human induced, such as an oil spill; natural, such as a decline in available food because of severe storms; or a combination of the two. This is one of the reasons that it is so important for us to also monitor the seabirds on this long journey.

A Galápagos storm-petrel

Galápagos storm-petrels are found far out at sea feeding on small crustaceans, halobates (the only marine insect), fish, and jellyfish at the ocean's surface. They breed on the remote and protected Galápagos Islands, which have few predators. Their populations at the moment appear to be stable.

AUGUST

Almost a month has passed. During the past weeks we recorded more than two hundred sightings of dolphin schools or whales and counted many hundreds of seabirds. This evening I treat myself to some time alone, something that is hard to find living on a 75-meter (222-foot) ship with thirty-six other people. I go up to one of the open decks to relax in my hammock. Glittering stars fill the sky. One shooting star zips through the darkness, leaving a long, brilliant trail. Night skies are spectacular out on the open ocean, where there is no light pollution. The Milky Way looks like a long, hazy cloud. When I look through my binoculars it becomes millions of specks of twinkling light. The breeze is warm and soft—a truly beautiful night.

NEARER THE EQUATOR

8°39′ N, 126°00′ W

As we continue south-west, we encounter many schools of spotted and spinner dolphins. Most of the schools are small, made up of maybe fifty to one hundred animals. Some schools are mixed, containing both species. The dolphins seem to be quite shy, not readily approaching the ship. Since these two species are usually curious and will come to investigate ships, this behavior is odd. Perhaps

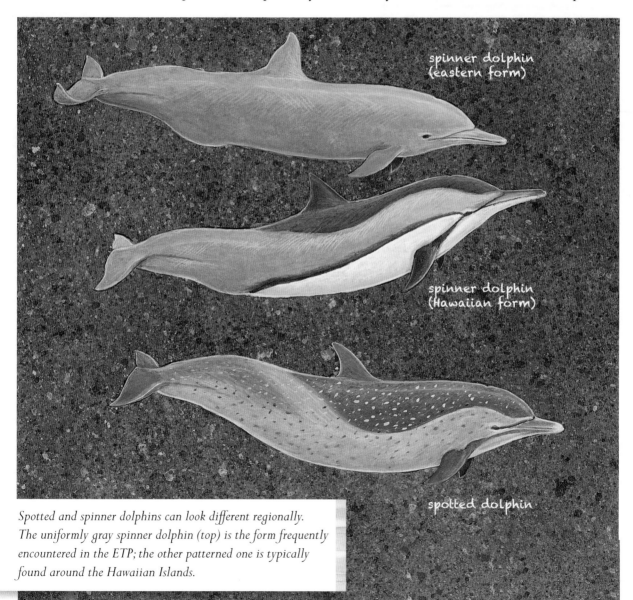

spinner dolphin
(eastern form)

spinner dolphin
(Hawaiian form)

spotted dolphin

Spotted and spinner dolphins can look different regionally. The uniformly gray spinner dolphin (top) is the form frequently encountered in the ETP; the other patterned one is typically found around the Hawaiian Islands.

they have been caught in the nets of purse seiners. Even if a dolphin is freed, the stress of being captured and released could change their behavior. So perhaps they now avoid ships.

The numbers of individual dolphins and sightings that we record over these months will help scientists determine the size and health of the dolphin stocks. It will help us find out if their population continues to recover now that tuna fishing practices have changed. Also our data will help set bycatch quotas, or the number of dolphins that can be accidentally killed yearly (still several thousand) in the tuna purse-seine fishery.

As a birder I have another task besides censusing seabirds. I count flying fish out to 100 meters (320 feet) from the ship. We count them because they are a major source of food for fish, birds, and dolphins in the ETP, so their numbers can give us an idea of the productivity of an area (if there is food available). The flying fish come in a variety of colors and shapes. There are "four-winged" flying fish and "two-winged" flying fish. The "wings" are modified fins that are used for gliding. They perform spectacular glides of several hundred meters. They even change course in midair or use their modified tail fin to wiggle on a wavelet to turn or extend the glide in an attempt to escape a fish, bird, or dolphin in hot pursuit. As the ship moves through the water, it flushes up the flying fish. Many hundred to several thousand two-winged flying fish erupt from the water in beautiful silvery sheets.

These graphs show the populations of spotted and spinner dolphins crashing in the early 1970s because of the tuna fishery. Now they appear stable but still with lower numbers than in the past. Courtesy NOAA Southwest Fisheries

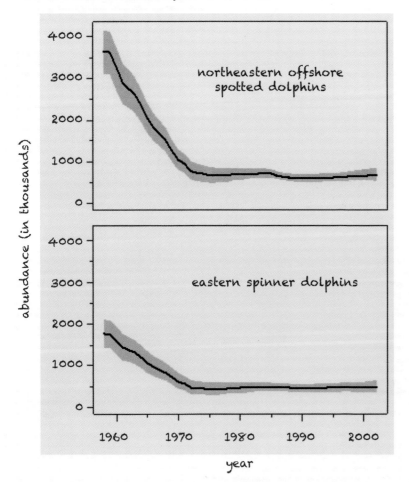

A close-up of five flying fish species. The California flying fish, the largest flying fish species, reaches forty-seven centimeters (eighteen inches) in length. Most of the adult flying fish in the ETP are between twenty and thirty-five centimeters (eight and fourteen inches) long.

LATE AUGUST
18°36' N, 156°23' W

The weather has become very warm, and the water temperature has increased dramatically. When we left California the sea surface water was around 19 degrees Celsius (60°F); now it's 28 degrees (85°F). The air feels thick and humid. The wind is warm in the mornings, hot midday, and pleasantly cool at night. Tropical summer can be lovely, but there are days when all I want to do is go inside to escape the heat, drink ice water, and sit in my air-conditioned cabin.

As the months go on we all fall into the routine of being at sea: working from dawn to dusk and eating meals at set times. I like this predictable routine for these months. My life on land is very different, with my days not following a predictable pattern.

Now we are off the island chain of Hawaii, heading for our first port call. I keep seeing odd large splashes in the distance, and I wonder what is making them. Finally the animal launches itself out of the water near me: a manta ray.

Manta rays commonly leap out of the water, but it is unclear why. Some possibilities are to communicate, to make a sexual display, or to rid themselves of parasites. Manta rays are ancient fish with cartilage rather than bones. Although related to sharks, manta rays filter plankton rather than eating meat. The largest manta ray on record was 7.6 meters (25 feet) and weighed 2,300 kilos (5,100 pounds).

AUGUST—HONOLULU, HAWAII

21°3' N, 157°8' W

This morning everyone wakes up early to watch as we come into port in Honolulu. We smell the land as we approach. The mountains of Oahu (one of the main islands in the Hawaiian Islands) look so green, and the city appears so large and busy after the solitude of the sea. I will spend the next days riding a bike around the city, going swimming, and hiking in Oahu's lush tropical mountains. It will be great to walk more than the 222 feet of the ship. I get restless at sea even though I can exercise regularly in the ship's small gym. (We don't swim at sea because sharks are attracted to anything that sits in the water in one location for too long, even in the open ocean.)

★ Honolulu

Honolulu harbor: the sight of skyscrapers, cars, and greenery is almost overwhelming.

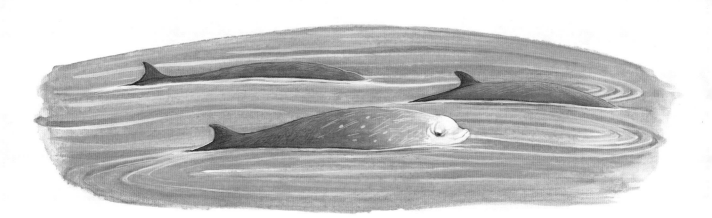

SEPTEMBER—BACK AT SEA
15°10′ N, 154°40′ W

After four days in port, we leave Hawaii and head southeast. In a few days we are just north of the equator. It's a calm day. We are in extremely deep water: 3,000 meters (10,000 feet), or close to two miles deep.

The sea appears empty.

Suddenly three brown-backed creatures roll up in front of the ship. Their backs are broad, with a small dorsal fin set toward the tail of each animal.

"Hey, those are beaked whales! STOP!" yells Jim, the marine mammal biologist.

Cornelia calls the bridge and asks them to slow the ship down.

We rush for our cameras as the three whales breathe slowly at the surface. *Click, click, click,* go the camera shutters. We try to photograph all the marine mammals we see. Later we will use photos to identify individuals, regional groups that look different from each other, and difficult-to-identify species.

One of the beaked whales is larger than the others and has a heavily scarred body and a mottled white head. It's a male. All three whales have a weirdly shaped head and a beak: they are Cuvier's beaked whales. Suddenly the animals disappear, diving as the ship drifts closer to them. Found far offshore, beaked whales are incredibly deep divers that eat mostly squid. Cuvier's beaked whales hold the world record for deep dives. They can dive to 1,900 meters—that's more than 6,000 feet, longer than a mile—and remain under water for over an hour!

How I imagine a pair of Cuvier's beaked whales look when swimming downward through the clear blue water on a deep dive. Males rake each other with their teeth when competing for females. Their bodies become covered with white scratches and scars. Their heads become paler with age. Cuvier's beaked whales are small whales—only about six meters (twenty feet) long.

Beaked whales are hard to see; rarely does one glimpse more than a back and dorsal fin. Several species are known only from carcasses or skulls that have washed ashore. They are one of the least known and most mysterious of the large mammals that inhabit the deep ocean.

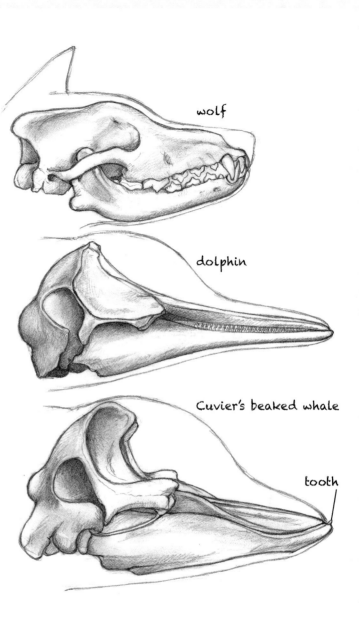

wolf

dolphin

Cuvier's beaked whale

tooth

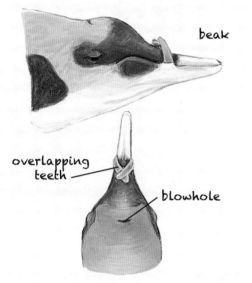

beak

overlapping teeth

blowhole

The head of a species of beaked whale called strap-toothed whale shows how the male's two teeth, or tusks, grow to curve over the beak and cross each other, preventing the whale from opening its mouth very far. Beaked whales feed by suction, like slurping squid through a straw.

These skulls (not to scale) show the differences between the skulls of two odontocetes and a familiar terrestrial carnivore, the wolf. Note that the only tooth visible on the male Cuvier's beaked whale's skull is the tiny one at the end of the lower jaw. Unlike the teeth of the strap-toothed whale, these teeth remain tiny. In all species of beaked whales, these teeth or tusks are thought to be used only for fighting.

Juan Fernandez petrels soar in front of an approaching rain squall.
They are the most common petrel that we see in the ETP. They breed
only on the Juan Fernandez Islands off of Chile.

END OF SEPTEMBER
8°53' N, 148°17' W

The weather has been overcast and windy the last couple of days. It's not much fun to work in these conditions. I scurry inside as soon as the first of my four two-hour shifts is over.

The ITCZ, or intertropical convergence zone, where north equatorial and equatorial countercurrents meet, can be squall-filled and stormy. The star is our location.

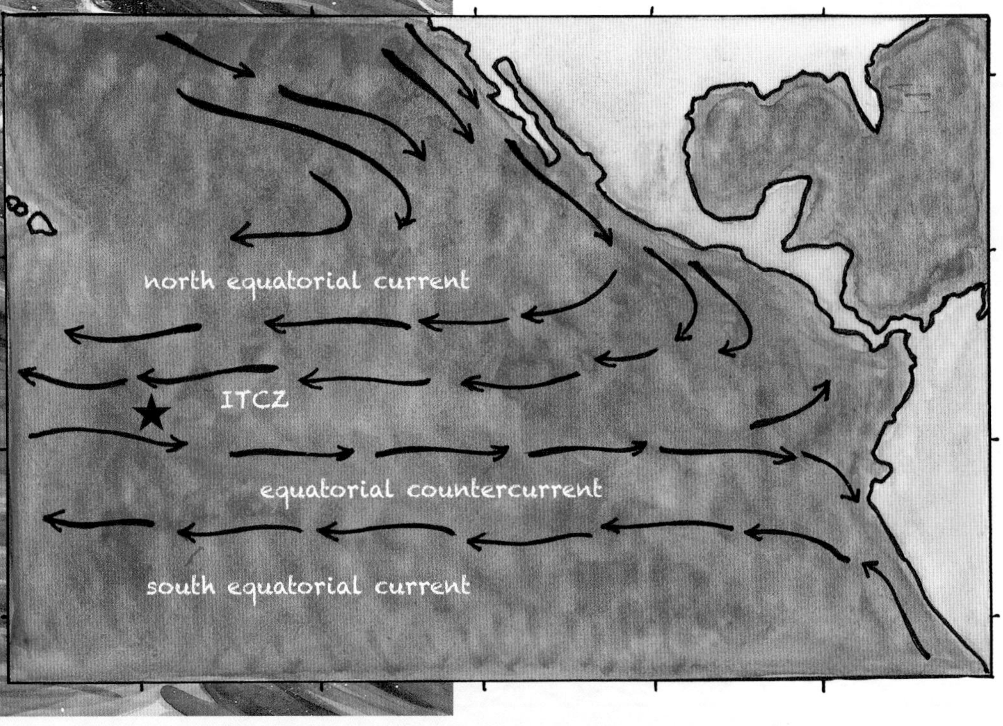

north equatorial current

ITCZ

equatorial countercurrent

south equatorial current

There's a little corner in the ship's lab where I sit and paint. I have started to spend so much time at sea that I have become used to painting even when the ship bounces and rocks from wind and waves. But I do tape my brush-cleaning water jar to the table so it won't topple over. Having my paintings to work on makes time at sea pass rapidly: I always have something to do on days when bad weather with high winds and rain keeps us from working, and in the evenings when my work day is finished. Other folks work on their own projects, such as writing scientific papers, or they simply relax and read, play cribbage (a game popular with sailors), or watch movies.

Duct tape can be used for anything! I use it at sea to tape my water jar to the desk.

ALONG THE EQUATOR
0°28' N, 121°0' W

The strong winds and rain squalls have kept us from working or seeing much for the past few days. But today the horizon is clear and crisp, and we are busy spotting many schools of spotted and spinner dolphins.

We also see several Bryde's (pronounced brooda's) whales. Bryde's whales are in the group called the mysticetes, or the baleen whales, which means they have no teeth; instead they have baleen plates in their mouth that filter plankton and small schooling fish. Bryde's whales are one of the few baleen whales we see in the deep tropical ocean.

A distant school of spinner dolphins, some spinning, with some whale blows nearby.

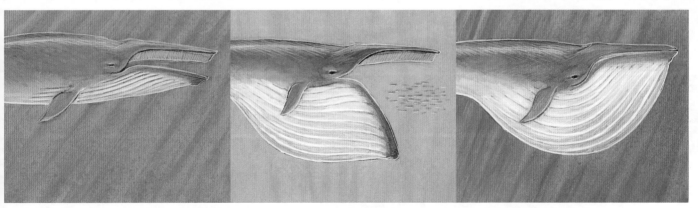

How a Bryde's whale might look feeding underwater. The baleen plates hang down from the upper jaw, and the throat grooves expand as the whale feeds. With its tongue it then pushes out the excess water through the baleen plates and strains out the fish and krill.

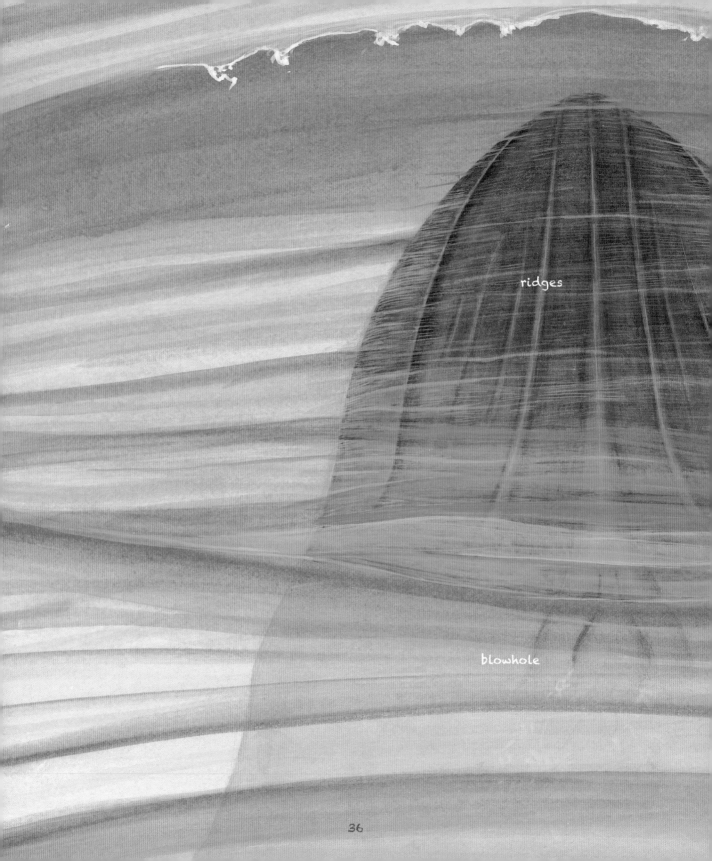

ridges

blowhole

Looking down from the flying bridge as a Bryde's whale rises to the surface to breathe. A thin layer of tropical blue water gives it a ghostly appearance. The distinctive head ridges and the closed blowhole are easily visible through the clear water. Bryde's and blue whales are the most common baleen whales we encounter in these deep tropical waters.

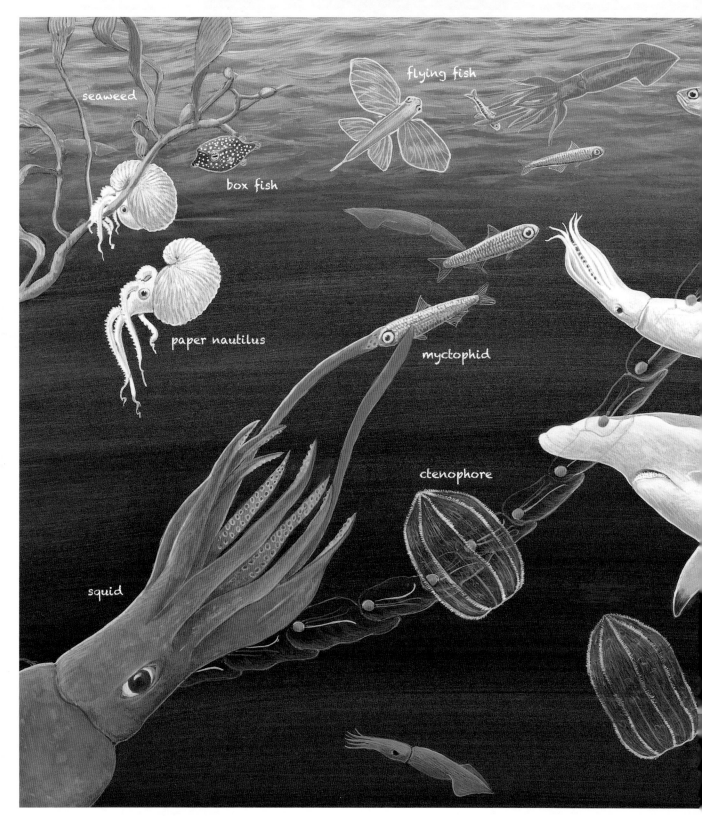

seaweed

flying fish

box fish

paper nautilus

myctophid

ctenophore

squid

flying fish

chain salp

pelagic red crab

hammerhead
shark

blue shark

Each night an hour after sunset, we conduct a sampling station where we gather various types of small surface-feeding animals. Bright lights shine down from above into the water to attract animals that vertically migrate at night from the depths to the ocean's surface. At dawn they return to the deep. Some of these animals are small lantern fish (myctophids) with light organs along the sides of their body. With dip nets we try to collect the smaller animals and store them for various scientists' studies. After the cruise the scientists will identify the species of each sample to understand their distribution and demographics (age and sex) in the deep Pacific. Long chains of salps and glittering ctenophores—mostly clear invertebrates (animals that lack a backbone)—float past. As we collect our water samples and do several net tows, sharks frequently swim past the ship. They are lured by all the activity and feed on the squid and fish attracted to the lights.

A squid's-eye view of what the ocean looks like at night when lit up by the ship's spotlights. Like the sharks, squid come to feed on fish and sometimes other squid. At times even large Humboldt squid rise to the surface near the ship. They are over a meter and a half (five feet) long. Squid are a major food for many species of marine mammals and seabirds.

ALMOST HALFWAY
2°42′ S, 97°12′ W

On Sundays when the weather is sunny and calm, we have a cookout on the back deck. If we are lucky, a scientist or crew member has caught a fish such as a mahi-mahi and donated it to the cooks. Dinner is cooked on a big gas grill, with hamburgers, veggie burgers, shish kebabs, corn on the cob, and hot dogs. In addition to the grilled food there is potato salad, several different kinds of coleslaw, chips and dips, and pies or cookies. I always enjoy the cookouts—sitting out on the back deck in the light breeze, watching the ocean swish by and chatting with my fellow shipmates.

The next day we continue to run along the equator, heading for our next port call in Ecuador. Along the way we encounter small numbers of dolphins and some blue whales with calves.

Along the coast of

Orcy, one of the cooks, grills fish and hamburgers for our outdoor feast.

Ecuador I see many soaring frigatebirds. Huge birds with a 2.3-meter (7.5-foot) wingspan, frigatebirds are robbers. They often feed by klepto-parasitizing, which means they chase other birds to force them to throw up their fish, which the frigate then eats. They also dip

and pluck fish and other creatures from the surface of the water. I watch a frigatebird pluck a sea snake from the water and am surprised. Sea snakes are quite poisonous.

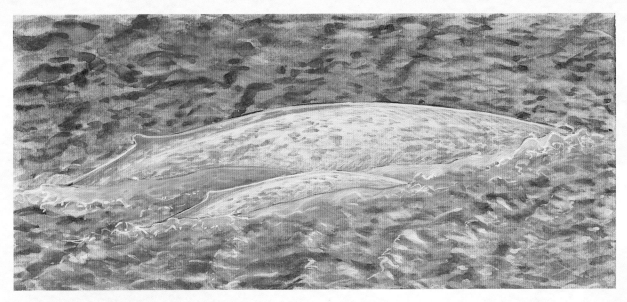

A blue whale cow and tiny calf. Not much is known about blue whales far from shore. These sightings are important to understand their distribution. We take many photos. Each blue whale's pattern and dorsal fin is unique, like a fingerprint, so individuals can be recognized. Although these whales are enormous at more than twenty-five meters (ninety feet) they have tiny dorsal fins placed far back on their bodies.

Frigatebirds are one of the birds purse-seine fishermen look for. They soar very high, so they can be spotted from many miles away as they circle over a tuna-dolphin school. The frigatebirds are looking for birds that are feeding over the dolphins and tuna.

OCTOBER—
MANTA, ECUADOR
01°05′ S, 80°40′ W

The busy fishing port of Manta, Ecuador. A crane unloads a net full of tuna from a purse seiner. Note the covered helicopter on the ship's upper deck.

We arrive in Manta early in the morning. We need to resupply our food stores and refuel the ship, so we stop in a variety of ports on these long trips. We have a long wait to clear customs and immigration. By late afternoon we are free to leave the ship. Everyone disperses in small groups for the four days we will be in port. I head south from Manta to a small town on the coast near a national park, where I plan to bird watch

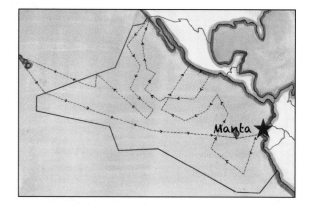

and sketch. Others head to the Andes for the cooler climate that high mountains provide.

Close to 1,600 bird species have been recorded in the tiny country of Ecuador. It is a bird lover's paradise with strange species everywhere. I see three favorites while bird watching: a colorful motmot, a laughing falcon, and a secretive ant shrike. The motmot is frequently called *pajaro reloj* (in Spanish pronounced *pah-HArro ray-LO*), or clock bird, because it flicks its long tail back and forth like a clock's pendulum; the laughing falcon is named for its loud laughing call; and the antshrike is in a group of birds called the ant birds because some species follow army ant swarms to feed on the insects the army ants scare up.

Ecuador lives up to its reputation. During my four days of bird watching I see well over a hundred species of birds. I plan to return for a longer visit next year.

blue-crowned motmot

laughing falcon

collared antshrike

Birds not to scale relative to each other.

43

BACK TO SEA
13°21' S, 90°1' W

When we return to the ship, we head even farther south of the equator, to the southern edge of our study area, before we turn north to begin our slow journey home.

Daily, the clouds amaze me. The water is a deep blue, the sky pale, dotted and banded with an ever-growing and changing array of clouds: cirrus, stratus, and the huge, puffy cumulus. In the early morning or early evening they take on a myriad of shapes and colors. They transform and move almost as if they are alive. I try to paint them.

NOVEMBER—
TWO-THIRDS COMPLETED

12°33′ N, 109°4′ W

It is afternoon. We chug along our track line at a steady ten knots, our standard survey speed. The air is hot and humid, 32 degrees Celsius (90°F). We all appreciate the shade of the canopy. The six marine mammal scientists have rotated through several shifts, each spending forty minutes standing at a set of big eyes on one side of the ship, then moving to the center to be the data recorder, followed by a third forty-minute stretch at the second pair of big eyes—a two-hour shift in total—then a break. I spend my two-hour shift scanning and watching for birds.

We begin to see more flocks of birds on the horizon, a sign that we have entered a productive area. I am busy trying to keep track of the flocks in the distance and individual birds flying by the ship.

The marine mammal scientists carefully look under the flocks for signs of dolphins. "Dolphins!" shouts

Mike, the other birder, takes a break and reads (or naps) in a lounge chair on the "steel beach," which is what we often call the sunny deck.

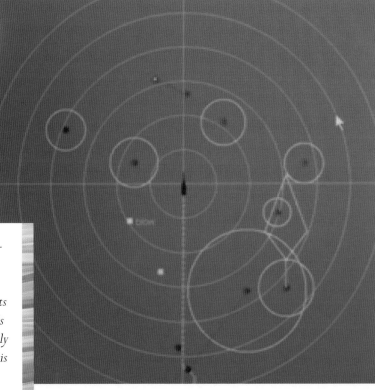

The map that tracks dolphin and whale sightings. Each red dot represents a sighting or a resighting of an animal or group of animals. The small circles and diamond around the dots are the zones of probability, where the animals are most likely to be resighted. The large, evenly spaced circles are each a mile apart. The ship is in the center of the circles.

A distant bird flock looks like a swarm of gnats flying over the ocean in front of the clouds. I look through the big eyes to begin counting and identifying the birds in the flock.

Cornelia. "I have dolphins at twenty degrees left, 0.3 reticles [a distance measurement that is in the eyepiece of the big eyes], moving 270 degrees at four knots under that chicken ranch!" (*Chicken ranch* is our slang for a big bird flock.) This information tells us the distance the dolphins are from the ship and describes the direction and speed they are traveling relative to the ship. The dolphins are still three miles away.

Ernesto enters the information Cornelia provided into a computer that has a tracking program; the program then creates a map. If the dolphins are distant and the conditions are not good when the ship turns, it's easy to lose sight of them. The tracking program gives the scientists an idea of where to look again for the dolphins.

"Can we come thirty degrees left, please?" Ernesto asks the bridge crew.

We turn and we're on

sooty tern

brown booby

white tern

south polar skua

Kermadec petrel

wedge-tailed shearwater

spotted dolphin

spinner dolphin

Juan Fernandez petrel

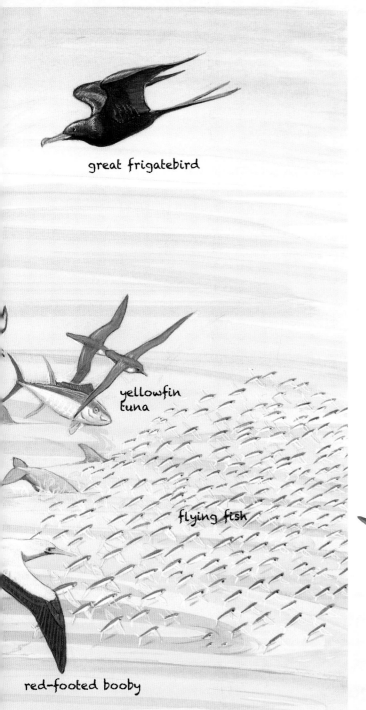

great frigatebird

yellowfin tuna

flying fish

red-footed booby

the chase. Tension and excitement mounts. As we approach, we see scores of birds and dolphins.

It is a feeding frenzy. A school of flying fish erupts from the water, trying to escape. There is a whirl of activity in the air above the splashing of the dolphins and tuna. So much is going on, it's hard to see it all. This is one of the great sights in the ETP.

A school of yellowfin tuna feeds on a huge school of flying fish. The flying fish try to escape the predators below them by gliding above the water on their modified fins, only to be snatched in midair by the birds. Dolphins leap, spin, and slap their tails. As the ship approaches, the dolphins turn toward it.

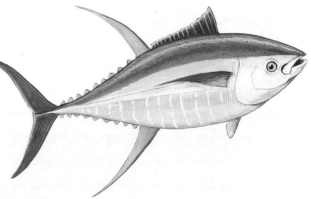

An adult yellowfin tuna, also known as ahi, can weigh more than four hundred pounds, although most of the fish we see are about half that size. Yellowfin tuna are one of the ETP fishing industry's main species.

Later I imagine and paint what the school of spotted and spinner dolphins with yellowfin tuna looks like in the water.

Spotted and spinner dolphins ride the bow wave. It's hard to believe that they don't experience sheer enjoyment in taking a ride.

Preparing to get a biopsy sample. Note the long orange tether attached to the modified arrow/bolt. The bolt can float in case the tether comes unattached or breaks. The bolt then can be retrieved with a long pole and net.

tip of a biopsy bolt

pencil for comparison

biopsy tray

When they reach the ship, the dolphins position themselves to be pushed forward by the pressure wave created by the moving ship. The dolphins almost jostle each other; apparently there is an optimal position to get the best ride. Everyone rushes down to the bow of the ship to take photos, take skin biopsy (tissue) samples, or to simply watch the action.

Shannon, my cabin-mate, leans over the side of the ship armed with a small crossbow. *PSSHT!*—she shoots a bolt at a dolphin as it surfaces to breathe. At the tip of the bolt there's a small cylinder with a sharp cutting edge. She hopes that as the bolt bounces off the dolphin it will remove and capture in the cylinder a small plug of tissue (approximately the size of a pencil eraser), which will be analyzed after the cruise in a lab.

The bolt is tethered to the ship by a long nylon string. Shannon quickly pulls it in by the string and checks it—yes, she has something. She removes the tip and puts it in a tray designed for holding the samples before putting on a new tip and shooting again. Later the tissue sample will be divided

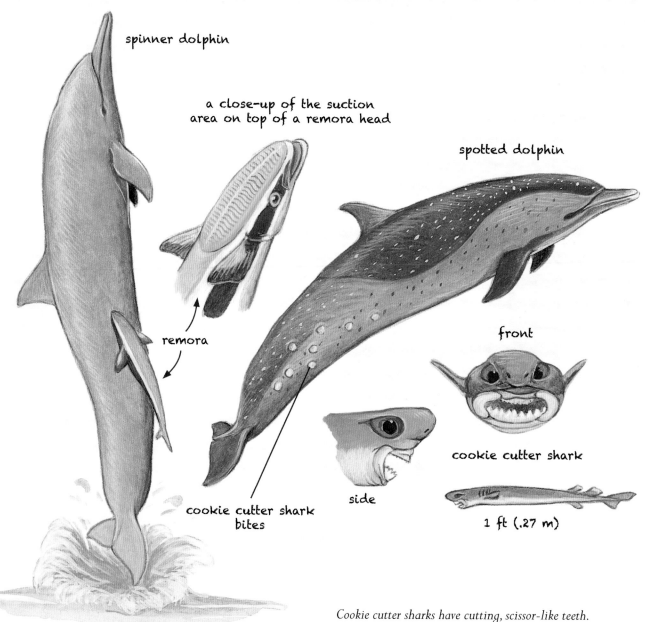

spinner dolphin

a close-up of the suction
area on top of a remora head

spotted dolphin

remora

front

cookie cutter shark
bites

side

cookie cutter shark

1 ft (.27 m)

Cookie cutter sharks have cutting, scissor-like teeth.
They bite, then twist, removing a chunk of skin.
These sharks are small, usually not more than a foot
long. Remoras are odd fish that have a suction cup–
like structure on the top of their head that they use
to attach themselves to dolphins and other marine
creatures, such as sharks. The remoras hitchhike to
clean up scraps of food when the dolphin or shark feeds.

I look down at the spotted dolphins from the bow. A cow (female dolphin) exhaling creates a long line of bubbles as she surfaces to breathe. Her small calf swims close to her side.

up and stored in a variety of ways. Surprisingly, the dolphins don't seem bothered by this activity and continue to ride the bow.

The biopsy dart probably doesn't feel like much to them. Several of the spotted dolphins have cookie cutter shark bites on their sides of 6.75 centimeters (3 inches) in diameter and 2.24 centimeters (1 inch) deep. A spinner dolphin spins, seemingly not bothered by the remora attached to its flank.

So what do biopsy samples tell us? When populations of marine mammals look too similar, scientists can identify the different groups by looking at their DNA (deoxyribonucleic acid) extracted from the tissue sample. They can also discover the dolphin's sex, whether it is pregnant, and whether the dolphins in a school are related. The blubber portion of the sample contains clues about chemical pollutants within the animal's environment. By looking at the toxins in marine mammal tissues, we may find out more about the health of an ecosystem.

When scientists began to look at biopsy samples from killer whales off the northwest coast of the United States, they discovered

Most dolphins are counter shaded, like these spotted dolphins, with a dark back and a pale underside. From below, the dolphins' pale bellies blend with the light from the surface; from above, their backs blend with the dark depths. This camouflage probably helps them pursue prey and escape predators such as killer whales.

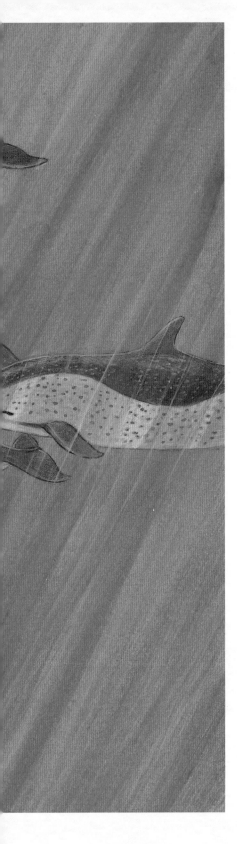

that some populations of killer whales had extremely high amounts of harmful toxins in their tissue. This may be contributing to their low breeding success.

As I lean over the edge of the ship to take pictures of the bow-riding dolphins, I hear high-pitched squeaks. The dolphins are calling to one another. They are social animals. I hear the whoosh of their numerous blows as they surface to breathe and the splashing of their bodies as they swim rapidly alongside the ship. They veer and move away, then turn to return to the bow.

One of the other NOAA research vessels I work on, the *David Starr Jordan,* has a bow chamber deep down in the ship with thick glass portholes. Getting there is a little creepy: I have to go through a heavy metal hatch that's hooked open with a chain, and down a metal ladder into a dark hold. But once I am there, it is wonderful. I lie on an old mattress to watch and listen to the bow-riding dolphins. From the bow chamber I see how they are oriented in the water, several layers deep— always swimming close to one another, moving up and down rapidly in three dimensions. They never bump into each other. This sight makes it even clearer to me that what we see on the surface is only a portion of the total numbers of dolphins in the school.

After spending more than an hour with us, the spotted and spinner dolphins begin to disperse and move away from the ship. It was a large group estimated to be at least 1,500 animals: 70 percent spotted dolphins, 30 percent spinner dolphins, 5 percent with calves. We took many photos and obtained sixteen biopsy samples. Biological fieldwork requires counting, identifying, observing, and recording in a way that the information can be analyzed later and the study replicated in future years to see if an animal population of concern has increased or decreased.

The map below shows eastern spinner dolphin sightings from several years of cruises. We can see that there are areas of high sighting concentrations. If we add to the map the time of year and the oceanographic measurements such as thermocline and sea surface temperature, we might find links between these factors and the dolphins. But first, it tells us what ocean conditions the dolphins like, and so where we might expect

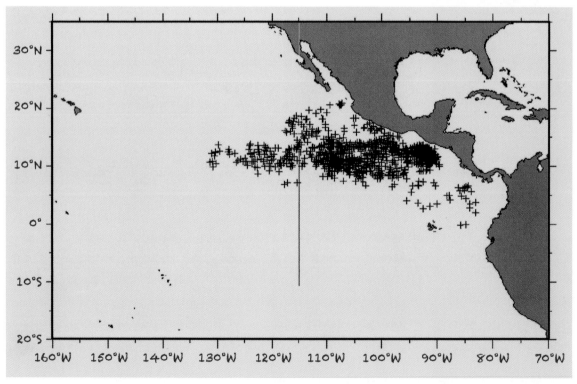

Courtesy Susan Chivers, NOAA SWFSC

Fishing gear can entangle animals. For example, a bottlenose dolphin is wrapped in monofilament (nylon) fishing line, a Minke whale (a small baleen whale) has put its head through a piece of fishing net, a humpback whale fluke is wrapped with line and fishing floats, and a sea turtle is entangled in a net.

to find them. If scientists discovered that spinner dolphins were concentrated in a particular area in the fall, making it easier for them to become part of the fishery bycatch, the area could be closed to fishing during that period and open in the spring when the dolphins were less numerous. On this cruise we are gathering the information we need in order to make these links between the dolphin and bird sightings and oceanographic data. This will not only help us understand the ecosystem better but also aid us in making good management decisions.

Besides purse seining, there are other dangers to dolphins and other marine life. Our oceans are becoming filled with plastic: plastic bags, balloons, cigarette lighters, combs, and cigarette butts that, if eaten, can make animals sick. Nets and monofilament line from fishing gear that break can fatally entangle marine animals. Occasionally we come across animals tangled in gear, particularly sea turtles. Frequently they have already died, but if not, we catch and free them.

Another month at sea has passed. We have now almost completed the third month of the cruise. Tomorrow will be our last port call before home.

The view from the Hotel la Posada in Manzanillo, where I stayed,
looking across the harbor to the old section of town. A great
kiskadee, a common tropical flycatcher, perches on
an ornamental plant in the foreground.

MANZANILLO, MEXICO: OUR FINAL PORT CALL

19°15′ N, 104°57′ W

As we cruise into the harbor we are greeted by hillsides covered with tropical vegetation and dotted with small, brightly colored houses. The air is hot and steamy. We have left the cool breezes of the ocean for another four-day stop in a tropical city to refuel and resupply. I need to refuel as well. When we are at sea, we work every day—no days off for weekends or holidays—unless it is very windy and stormy and we can't work. We do, though, celebrate birthdays and holidays such as Halloween and Thanksgiving. The cooks prepare a special meal, or we have a little party in the early evening after the day's work is completed and before night operations begin.

I spend part of my time in Manzanillo relaxing near the beach and swimming, followed by a brief bird-watching trip to the forest on the slopes of a nearby volcano, Volcán Fuego (Fire Volcano).

A NOVEMBER DAWN
15°49' N, 99°38' W

The time has passed so quickly that it's hard to believe it's November and that we've been at sea for more than three months. Now there is less than a month before we arrive home. We are off the coast of Mexico, where we see numerous schools of dolphins and many flocks of migrant and wintering seabirds. The ocean is littered with olive ridley sea turtles making their way either to or from their Mexican nesting beaches. In the distance they look like large floating coconuts until one lifts its head up to breathe or a waving flipper breaks the surface of the water.

Not only are there many migrant seabirds about for me to count, but because we are at sea during the fall—migration time for many birds—we frequently have lost and tired land birds perching on board. They are always unexpected and add a splash of color as they flit about the white and gray ship.

A prothonotary warbler, a neotropical migrant that breeds in the United States and winters in Mexico, Central America, and northern South America, takes a rest on the ship. I liked the contrast of this bright yellow bird perched below a winch.

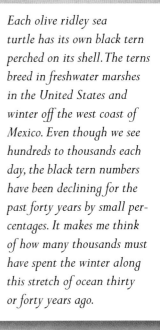

Each olive ridley sea turtle has its own black tern perched on its shell. The terns breed in freshwater marshes in the United States and winter off the west coast of Mexico. Even though we see hundreds to thousands each day, the black tern numbers have been declining for the past forty years by small percentages. It makes me think of how many thousands must have spent the winter along this stretch of ocean thirty or forty years ago.

The ship's jack staff is full.
Seven red-footed boobies
is just about its capacity.
These are the most pelagic,
or open ocean, of the boobies
frequently seen offshore.

Throughout the trip a squadron of boobies has flown along with us. These clever birds have learned that the ship flushes schools of flying fish, their favorite food. Red-footed boobies zoom over the water's surface in incredible flying chases, picking fish out of the air and gobbling them down. On the front of the ship is a small mast called the jack staff where the boobies like to perch. They are endlessly entertaining as they squabble to get the best spot, refusing to make room for one another. They poop everywhere, splattering the deck, making a mess for the crew to clean up. When they fly in front of the flying bridge, they bombard us. Booby poop is fishy smelling, sticky, and almost impossible to wash out of hair or clothes.

A red-footed booby chases a flying fish over the surface of the water. Another bird catches one in midair.

To me, striped dolphins are one of the most beautifully patterned dolphins. They are also incredibly acrobatic and fast. We call them streakers because of their ability to speed through the water, combined with their striped pattern. Frequently they make huge leaps and do somersaults. Here a calf porpoises alongside its mother.

CLOSER TO HOME
21°20′ N, 119°18′ W

The days are noticeably shorter, the shadows longer, and the air has a hint of fall in it.

Today is clear and calm, and we see two different schools of striped dolphins. Although striped, spotted, and spinner dolphins are closely related, striped dolphins don't generally associate with tuna and neither do they frequently bow ride. They are a bit shy. Today, though, one of the schools is quite easily approached and doesn't dash away from us. Still, we are only able to take photos of them. They are never close enough to biopsy.

The sun sets. The horizon is clear. Work is over for today. It's too dark to observe, but we remain on the flying bridge to chat. The sky turns pink, then orange. As the sun finally descends below the horizon, a brilliant greenish turquoise blue briefly flashes. The sun is gone. But we soon find that the day is not over. A series of long, sparkling streaks in the water suddenly appear, rushing toward the bow of the ship. It's a school of short-beaked common dolphins. In some plankton species a chemical reaction takes place when they are disturbed. The energy from the reaction is released as light: bioluminescence. Tonight the water is full of bioluminescent plankton. The dolphins catch the bow wave and move off and return, always leaving behind them a glittering green trail.

Since our toilets are flushed with seawater, if I flush the toilet in the dark it too will glitter with bioluminescent plankton.

NOVEMBER— OUR LAST WHALE SIGHTING

27°16′ N, 119°50′ W

The cruise is nearing an end; only a week left before we dock in San Diego. I begin to think of home. It's a slow day with few sightings.

Suddenly Jim yells "Sperm whales!" In the distance we see a series of low, puffy blows and long, straight backs with a hump toward the tail. Quickly we launch an inflatable power boat to get closer to the whales for both biopsy samples and photos. I join the crew going out. About thirty whales are spread out over a mile or two. We drive up behind one as it breathes. Because of the length and depth of their feeding dives—1,000 meters (over 3,000 feet) deep and forty-five minutes to an hour long—sperm whales must remain at the surface for about ten minutes to breathe to reoxygenate their blood.

We creep up to within 3 or 4 meters (12–15 feet) of an 18-meter (60-foot) whale and idle there. It is an odd creature, mostly head with some warts and nicks visible on the smooth parts of its skin. Behind the head the body is wrinkled. *Whoosh*— the blow cants off to the left. Sperm whales are one of the few asymmetrical animals in nature; their blow hole is located on the left of the immense head.

It has been ten minutes. The whale begins to rock forward, almost diving, gathering momentum; then it arches and rocks forward again, its head pointed straight down. As the whale descends, the fluke lofts into the air and Jim shoots. The dart bounces off the raised fluke and into the water. The whale disappears. We motor over to the floating dart and pick it up. A small plug of tissue remains in it. Of our four more attempts at tissue gathering, three are successful. Each time we get close to a whale I am filled with awe.

When the whales move away, we return to the ship. The boat is lifted aboard and secured into its deck cradle. Exhilarated and exhausted from our time out in the small boat, we head below decks for dinner and sleep.

The sperm whale's fluke is raised into the air as it straightens its body out into a near-vertical dive. The front of the whale's head is eighteen meters (sixty feet) below the surface of the water. There is a huge difference in water pressure from the head to the tail during such a dive. I wonder if the whales feel this pressure. A sperm whale blows in the background. Another whale begins its dive.

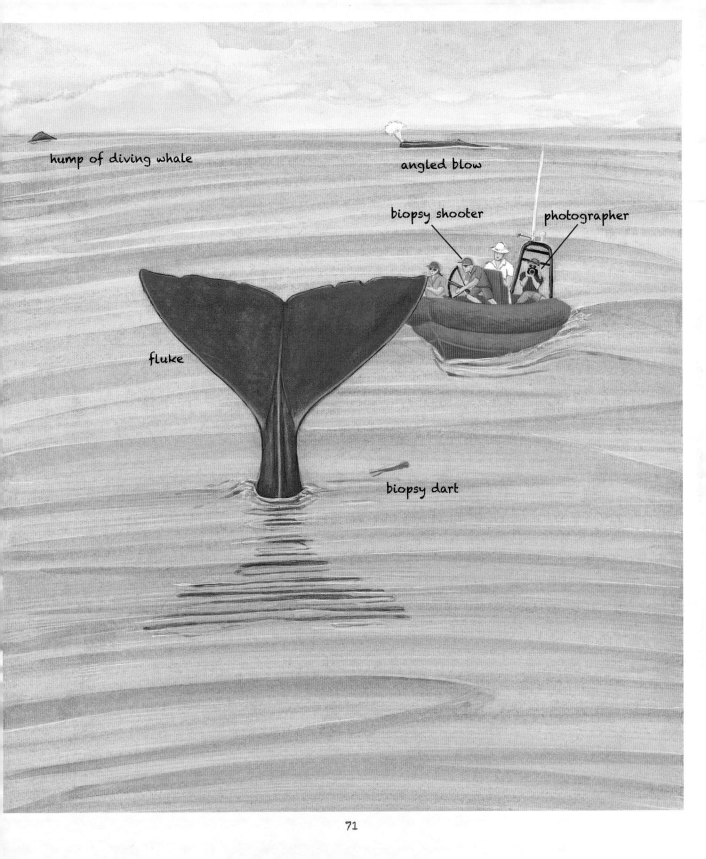

hump of diving whale

angled blow

biopsy shooter

photographer

fluke

biopsy dart

How I imagine a sperm whale feeds under water, although the depth, more than 320 meters (1,000 feet), could be too great for light to penetrate, so it would be too dark to see anything. Sperm whales maneuver by emitting clicks to echolocate: they "see" with sound. Squid, including giant squid, are a major component of their diet. Scientists know this not from observing the whales feed—it's too deep and dark—but from looking at the stomach contents of dead beached sperm whales. The beaks of squid are made of hard keratin that does not digest easily, so they remain in the whale's stomach long after the squid are eaten and the soft tissues digested. The squid emit a cloud of squid ink in an attempt to confuse the whale.

Arts and crafts for centuries were a means for sailors to fill their long days at sea. Scrimshaw, the engraving on bone or ivory with sharp tools followed by rubbing the lines with ink, became popular with sailors in the 1800s. Frequently they etched their designs on sperm whale teeth.

DECEMBER—
ALMOST HOME

30°32′ N, 118°42′ W

I t is the last day of the cruise; we are one day southwest of San Diego. The wind has a distinct bite— the early winter air is cool. The water temperature has dropped dramatically in the past week from around 27 (80°F) to 17 degrees Celsius (62°F). We left on the cruise in late summer, and now we head north into winter.

There are splashes off toward the horizon. Dolphins? Yes. They move quickly in a frothy group. Our heading (direction) will cross their path; no need to alter the ship's course in order to count them and get samples. I smile as they become more distinct. They are familiar friends from the north. Some of the dolphins are black streamlined torpedoes, lacking a dorsal fin. These are northern right whale dolphins. Others are prettily patterned with a bicolored dorsal fin: Pacific white-sided dolphins. I am surprised to see them here; I don't associate them with waters south of San Diego. Northern right whale dolphins are my favorite species of dolphin be-cause of their elegance, speed, and grace. The whole school turns and races for the bow and surrounds the front of the ship.

The dolphins swim along with us, leading us home.

northern right whale dolphin

Pacific white-sided dolphin

DECEMBER— SAN DIEGO
32°73′ N, 117° 17′ W

I t's early morning. We motor into San Diego harbor. There is an air of excitement and anticipation. Four months is a long time to be away from my home, friends, and family. But there is also a hint of nostalgia for the trip, for new friends made and unique experiences shared. I look forward to seeing and working with everyone in the future.

During the past months we recorded more than nine hundred groups of dolphins and whales, counted many thousands of individual seabirds and more than 150 flocks. I have so many memories: dolphins glowing in the bioluminescence, a Bryde's whale surfacing in clear blue water, nights under the tropical stars, huge bird flocks swirling over feeding tuna and dolphins, and glimpses of Cuvier's beaked whales.

Each year that I go out to explore this mysterious and wonderful ocean ecosystem far from shore, I learn or see something new and remarkable. It frequently takes years of data to understand what is happening in this complex field: Is a population of dolphins increasing or decreasing? What seabirds and marine mammals are affected by plastic and pollution? By a fishery? Or by the changes in our climate? Only with long-term monitoring can these things be discovered.

I hope others can journey out to the ETP long into our future to see spotted and spinner dolphins gracefully leap among schools of tuna while overhead flocks of wheeling and diving seabirds color the sky.

BALEEN a series of vertical keratin (a protein material similar to fingernails) plates in the mouth of some whales, used as a strainer during feeding.
pp. 34, 35, 36–37, 59

BEAKED WHALE a group of odd, little-known deep-sea toothed whales.
pp. 29, 30, 31

BEAUFORT SCALE a scale to describe wind speed based on sea conditions, traditionally numbered 0–12.
p. 14

BIOLUMINESCENCE a chemical reaction in organisms, in this case particularly plankton, that lets off energy as light.
pp. 68–69

BIOPSY a small tissue sample for study and diagnostics.
pp. 53, 55, 58, 70

BRIDGE the deck or area of a ship where the controls are located, e.g., steering and navigation equipment.
pp. 8–9

BYCATCH animals caught in a fishery that are not part of the target species, e.g., dolphins, birds, turtles.
pp. 25, 59

CELSIUS a temperature scale usually used by scientists in which 0 degrees is freezing and 100 degrees is boiling.
pp. 27, 46, 74

CHLOROPHYLL a molecule found in almost all plants and algae that absorbs light and is integral in the process of photosynthesis. Simply, it helps to create energy from light.
p. 13

CIRRUS a type of high, wispy hairlike cloud called mares' tails by sailors.
pp. 44–45

CUMULUS big puffy clouds that are constantly seen at the horizon in the ETP. Sometimes they are storm clouds: thunderheads.
pp. 44–45

DORSAL FIN the fin on the back of a dolphin or fish that helps prevent the animal from rolling, perhaps particularly during sudden turns.
pp. 16, 29, 31, 41

DNA deoxyribonucleic acid, the building block of life, the molecule that makes up our genes.
p. 55

ECHOLOCATION Animal sonar. Animals emit calls and listen for and receive the echo of the call as it bounces off other animals or objects in the environment, "seeing" with sound.
pp. 72–73

ECOLOGY the branch of biology that deals with the relations of animals to one another and to their physical surroundings
p. 5

ECOSYSTEM an independent grouping of organisms of the same habitat that work together with all the physical aspects of the environment, such as wind, weather, tides, and currents.
pp. 5, 7, 10, 13, 55, 59, 77

FLUKE the tail fins of a whale or dolphin.
p. 71

FAHRENHEIT/F° a temperature scale on which 32 degrees is freezing and 212 degrees is boiling.
pp. 27, 46, 74

KERATIN a hard protein substance like that of fingernails.
pp. 72–73

LATITUDE location on earth either north or south of the equator. The horizontal lines running east to west on a map or globe. A degree is equal to sixty nautical miles (a nautical mile is 1.15 miles). Degrees are indicated by °. Each degree is divided into sixty units called minutes, indicated by '. Each minute is one nautical mile. Minutes can be further divided into sixty seconds. Each is 0.016 nautical miles and is indicated by ". For example: 13°49'33" N.
p. 6

LIGHT POLLUTION Bright lights from cities and towns wash out the night sky so one can't see the stars. Observatories where people study the stars are found in remote areas far from cities to avoid the problem of light pollution.
pp. 22–23

LONGITUDE location on earth either east or west. These are the lines that run from north pole to south pole on a map or globe. Longitude is difficult to calculate because the distance of degrees, minutes, and seconds (see latitude) change as one moves north or south from the equator because of the curvature of the earth. A degree starts as sixty nautical miles at the equator, at latitude 45° is about forty-two nautical

miles, and finally becomes zero at the poles. The combination of latitude and longitude can pinpoint an exact location on earth.
p. 6

MESS the dining area on a ship. From Old English, a term for a piece of food.
pp. 8–9

MILKY WAY the galaxy that our solar system is in. It is made up of billions of stars, which on clear nights can be seen as a long pale swath in the night sky.
pp. 22–23

MYSTICETES the baleen whales, including humpback, blue, Bryde's, and fin whales.
p. 34

NATURALIST a scientist who studies animals through observation rather than experimentation.
p. 5

ODONTOCETES the toothed whales, including dolphins, porpoises, sperm whales, and beaked whales.
pp. 20, 31

PELAGIC having to do with the open ocean beyond the continental shelf.
pp. 18–19, 38–39, 64

PLANKTON small drifting organisms (plants, animals or bacteria).
pp. 12, 13

PORT the left side of a ship.
p. 15

PURSE SEINE a type of fishing net. A purse seiner is a fishing boat.
pp. 5, 10, 11

QUOTA the amount of fish or bycatch allowed to be caught by law in a managed fishery.
p. 25

RETICLE a distance measurement on the "big eye" binoculars.
p. 47

SALINITY the amount of dissolved salt in water.
p. 13

SCRIMSHAW an etching technique on bone or ivory.
p. 73

SQUALL a localized storm bringing wind and rain.
pp. 32–33, 34

STARBOARD the right side of a ship.
p. 15

STOCK a defined population.
p. 25

STRATUS a layer formation cloud.
pp. 44–45

THERMOCLINE where two water masses meet often with a large temperature change.
pp. 13, 58

TRANSECT in this case a predetermined line or course that the ship follows.
pp. 15, 21

Acknowledgments

Many people helped with the creation of this book. First I want to thank my boss, Dr. Lisa Ballance. Without the opportunity to spend months at sea working for NOAA's Southwest Fisheries Science Center's Protected Resources Division, I would never have had the ability to write and illustrate this book. I thank Larry Spear, who in 1990 introduced me to the wonders of the ETP. I thank the NOAA officers and crew of the RV *MacArthur II* and the RV *David Starr Jordan*: in particular Captain Greg Hubner, Scott Hill, Lacey O'Neal, Dave LaPointe, Dave Hermanson, João Alves, Chico Gomez, and Kevin Lackey. Over the past eight years, both ships became second homes for me.

I also want to thank all the biologists I have spent time with at sea, in particular David Ainley, Eric Archer, Jay Barlow, Isabel Beasley, Dawn Breese, Jim Carretta, Lilian Carswell, Susan Chivers, Jim Cotton, Chris Cutler, Dru Devlin, Lisa Etherington, Mike Force, Karin Forney, Denise Hardesty, Steve Howell, Jaime Janhcke, Heather Judkins, Carol Keiper, Nina Karnovsky, Kerry Kopitsky, Kirsten Lindquist, Shannon Lyday, Cornelia Oedekoven, Paula Olsen, Rich Pagen, Bob Pitman, Shannon Rankin, Katie Roberts, Richard Rowlett, Juan Carlos Salinas, Ernesto Vasquez, and Suzanne Yin.

Lisa Ballance, Dawn Breese, Margaret Brown, Nina and Max Karnovsky, Kevin Lackey, Hannah Nevins, Rebecca Norris-Webb, Lina Prairie, and Nancy Webb were careful readers and editors, making many helpful and insightful suggestions that greatly improved the book.

I thank Michelle Hester and Fiona Reid for having faith that I would finish.

I also thank PRBO Conservation Science for numerous opportunities to work at sea and Oikonos Ecosystem Knowledge for its support.

Last, I thank my editor, Ann Rider, for unending patience throughout the entire process.

Any inaccuracies in the information presented are entirely mine.